HarperCollins*Publishers*
1 London Bridge Street
London SE1 9GF

www.harpercollins.co.uk

HarperCollins*Publishers*
1st Floor, Watermarque Building, Ringsend Road
Dublin 4, Ireland

First published by HarperCollins*Publishers* 2022

1 3 5 7 9 10 8 6 4 2

Text © James Stewart 2022
Illustrations © K Roméy 2022

Hey Buddy Comics assert the moral right to be
identified as the authors of this work

A catalogue record of this book is
available from the British Library

ISBN 978-0-00-853084-6

Printed and bound in Latvia

MIX
Paper from
responsible sources
FSC™ C007454

contents

To Nina,
Oliver, Ada and
Penny. My forever pack.
James

To L, KC, Jack and Caven
for being my motivation
to get out of bed.
K

introduction

In the introduction to our first book, *dinosaur therapy*, I said I thought that the loneliness, depression and anxiety caused by the COVID-19 pandemic were part of the reason why our mental-health-focused dinosaur comics took off so quickly. As I write this a year later and the pandemic continues, I do not think these issues are becoming the new normal; rather, I think they were always normal, and the pandemic has merely caused an increase both in their incidence and our need to talk about them. Every year more people live their lives with some kind of mental-health issue hanging over them. I hope that talking about these issues in a blunt and open way offers those people some brief catharsis.

dinosaur philosophy

While there are some comics in this book that touch on specific philosophical issues, in general they focus on philosophy in the sense of one's attitudes towards, and principles about, life. If I had to sum up briefly the dinosaur philosophy, I would do so thus:

Face the negatives in life with hope and a sense of humour. Welcome the positive sides of life without cynicism and with an open heart. Remember that however annoying and frustrating people might sometimes seem, they are all we have.*

I regularly fail to live up to these principles, but what kind of principles would they be if they were easy to follow? On that positive note, enjoy the comics!

James

*Okay, we also have dogs.

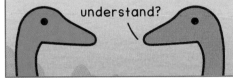

13

18

19

21

23

33

34

37

philosophy
of mind

how do i think?

45

51

53

55

59

ethics

how should i live?

75

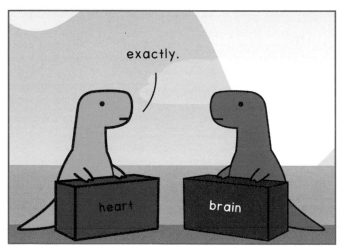

76

81

82

83

85

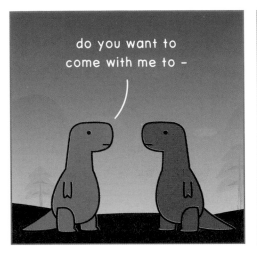

87

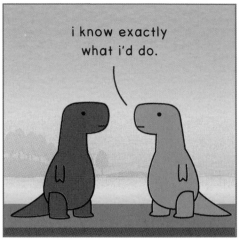
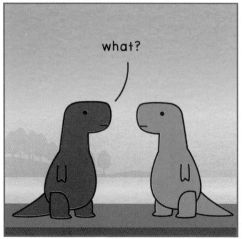

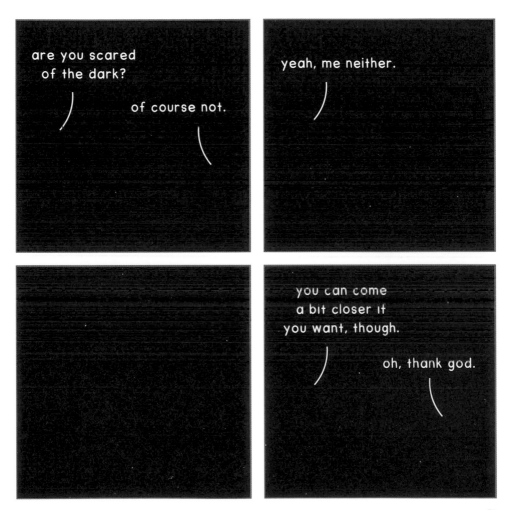

91

93

you're worthy!

why are you doing that?

sometimes people up there hear the call of the void.

i'm just offering some balance.

you're valid!

95

political philosophy

how should we live?

aesthetics

what is beauty?

it's okay to do nothing.

because sometimes
doing nothing ...

... is doing something.

133

138

143